CONTENTS

Words in the glossary appear in **bold** type the first time they are used in the text.

WELCOME TO THE EVERGLADES

There's no other park in the United States like Everglades National Park! Found on the southern tip of Florida, Everglades National Park keeps around one-fifth of the Everglades safe. While this may seem small, Everglades National Park is still about 2,400 square miles (6,216 sq km)!

The Everglades has been a popular, or well-visited, area since long before it was ever a national park. So, grab your boots and get ready to explore one of America's great wetlands!

Everglades National Park is about an hour away from Miami, Florida.

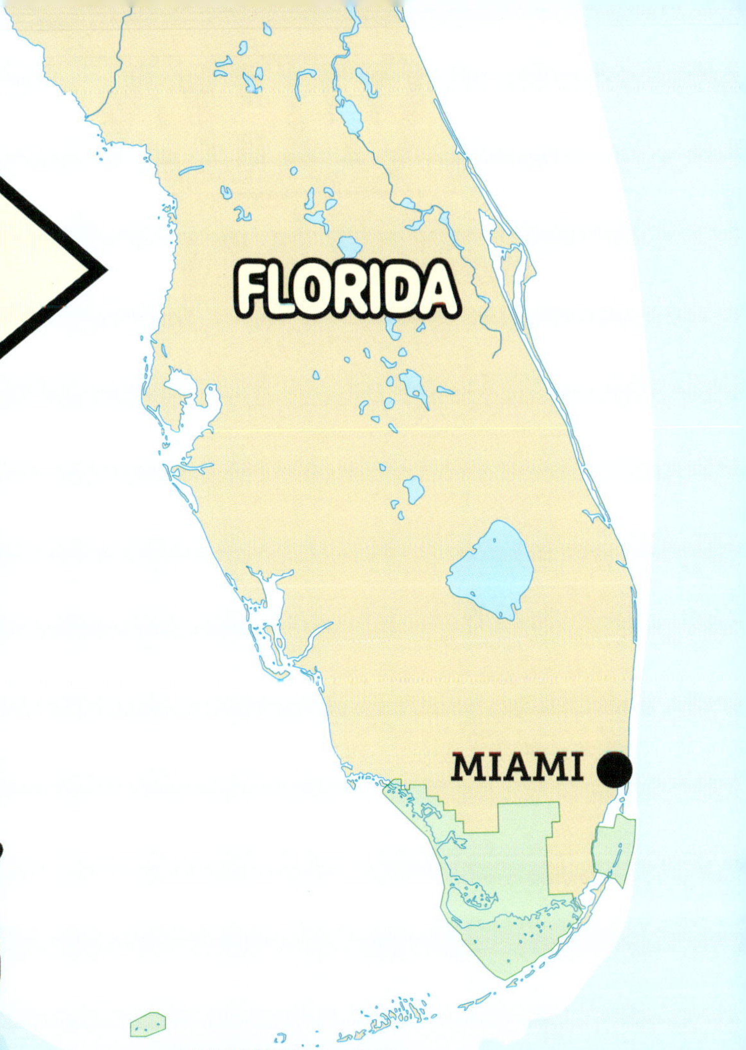

MORE TO KNOW

The Everglades is the largest **subtropical** wilderness in the United States! A wilderness is a piece of land without people living on it that is left to grow wild.

WHAT DOES IT MEAN?

The Florida Everglades, including the land in the national park, is the only place in the world called "everglades." But what does "everglades" mean? A glade is an open grassy area in a forest or **swamp**. "Ever" can refer to something that goes on for always, or forever. This makes the Everglades a field of grass that seems to go on forever.

Before the Europeans gave the Everglades this name, though, the Seminole Native Americans called the Everglades "pa-hay-okee," or "grassy waters."

The Everglades are the biggest **breeding** grounds in North America for wading birds.

MORE TO KNOW

Conservationist Marjory Stoneman Douglas said, "There are no other Everglades in the world. They are one of the **unique** regions of the earth. Nothing anywhere else is like them."

DRAINING THE EVERGLADES

During the 1800s, some people started trying to drain water out of the Everglades. They wanted to use the land to build farms. About the same time, people were overhunting birds and other wildlife for their skin and feathers. Conservationists began to worry about the **ecosystem**.

To keep the Everglades safe, scientists asked the government to make part of the Everglades a state park. In 1916, nearly 2,000 acres (809 ha) of land in the Everglades was named Royal Palm State Park. By 1921, the state added more land, doubling the park's size.

Royal Palm State Park was the first state park in Florida. It would later become part of Everglades National Park.

MORE TO KNOW

Today, some Miccosukee Native Americans live on the northern border of Everglades National Park. Some of Seminole Native Americans, many of whom lived in the Everglades area from the 1700s until the mid-1800s, still live in southern Florida.

BECOMING A NATIONAL PARK

Even before part of Everglades became a national park, Congress recognized the area as land that needed to be protected, or kept safe. In 1934, the national park was authorized, or approved. It took a while to get the land, but, in 1947, Everglades National Park was officially established.

Today, visitors can learn about the special **habitats** protected there. These include the hardwood hammocks, which are stands of many kinds of trees, including mahogany. Mangrove forests also are found along rivers and streams in the area.

In Florida, it's illegal to cut down a mangrove tree without special written permission.

MORE TO KNOW

Mangrove trees can grow in both fresh and salty water. Their roots help keep soil from washing away and may often be homes for fish.

ESTUARIES

An estuary is a place where salty seawater from the ocean meets fresh water **inland**. Florida Bay is a popular estuary that many people visit in the park. However, it can be dangerous. Florida Bay is only 5 feet (1.5 m) deep or less and is covered in seagrass.

While it's possible to take a boat through the waterways, boaters need to be careful. With all the seagrass, it can be hard to tell how deep the water is!

MORE TO KNOW

One way to get around the Everglades is by traveling on a freshwater slough (SLOO), such as Taylor Slough or Shark River Slough. Sloughs are swampy rivers.

Visitors to the Everglades can go for a slog, or wet hike, through many of the park's sloughs.

WILDLIFE

Everglades National Park is filled with wildlife. Over 360 different species, or types, of birds live in the Everglades. More than 20 species of snakes also live in the Everglades. If you're looking for amphibians, the Everglades has many different species of frogs, salamanders, and newts.

The Everglades also has many larger animals. Manatees and Florida panthers can also be found in the park. You can spot alligators and crocodiles in Shark Valley, the Anhinga Trail, and Eco Pond.

If you see a wild animal on your trip, make sure to give it plenty of space!

MORE TO KNOW

Not every animal found in the Everglades is native to Florida. Many species, including Burmese pythons, are **invasive**.

ENDANGERED IN THE EVERGLADES

Many species in the Everglades are threatened or endangered. These are living things that are at risk of dying out and need special care to save. There are about 110 plant species growing in the park that are endangered. More than 20 endangered or uncommon animal species, including the snail kite, manatee, and alligator, are protected in the Everglades too.

There are conservation efforts in the park to **restore** the Everglades. Conservationists and park rangers work together to protect the park.

SNAIL KITE

FLORIDA BONNETED BAT

Florida bonneted bats and wood storks are two more kinds of endangered animals that live in the Everglades.

WOOD STORK

MORE TO KNOW

Around one-third of Everglades National Park is covered in water! The water in the Everglades is also closely **monitored** for changes.

AIRBOAT TOURS

Have you ever taken a ride on an airboat? Airboats are one of the best ways to get around Everglades National Park. At Everglades Safari Park, you can take an airboat ride and see a wildlife show!

Canoes and boats can also travel down all or part of the Wilderness Waterway. It's 99 miles (159 km) long. It usually takes around eight days to travel from one end of the trail to the other.

MORE TO KNOW

Airboats are boats with a flat bottom and a large, fanlike **propeller** on the back. They're used in shallow, or not deep, water where a propeller that goes under the water can't be used.

You should never feed or touch the animals in the wild. But, many people like to watch them from an airboat!

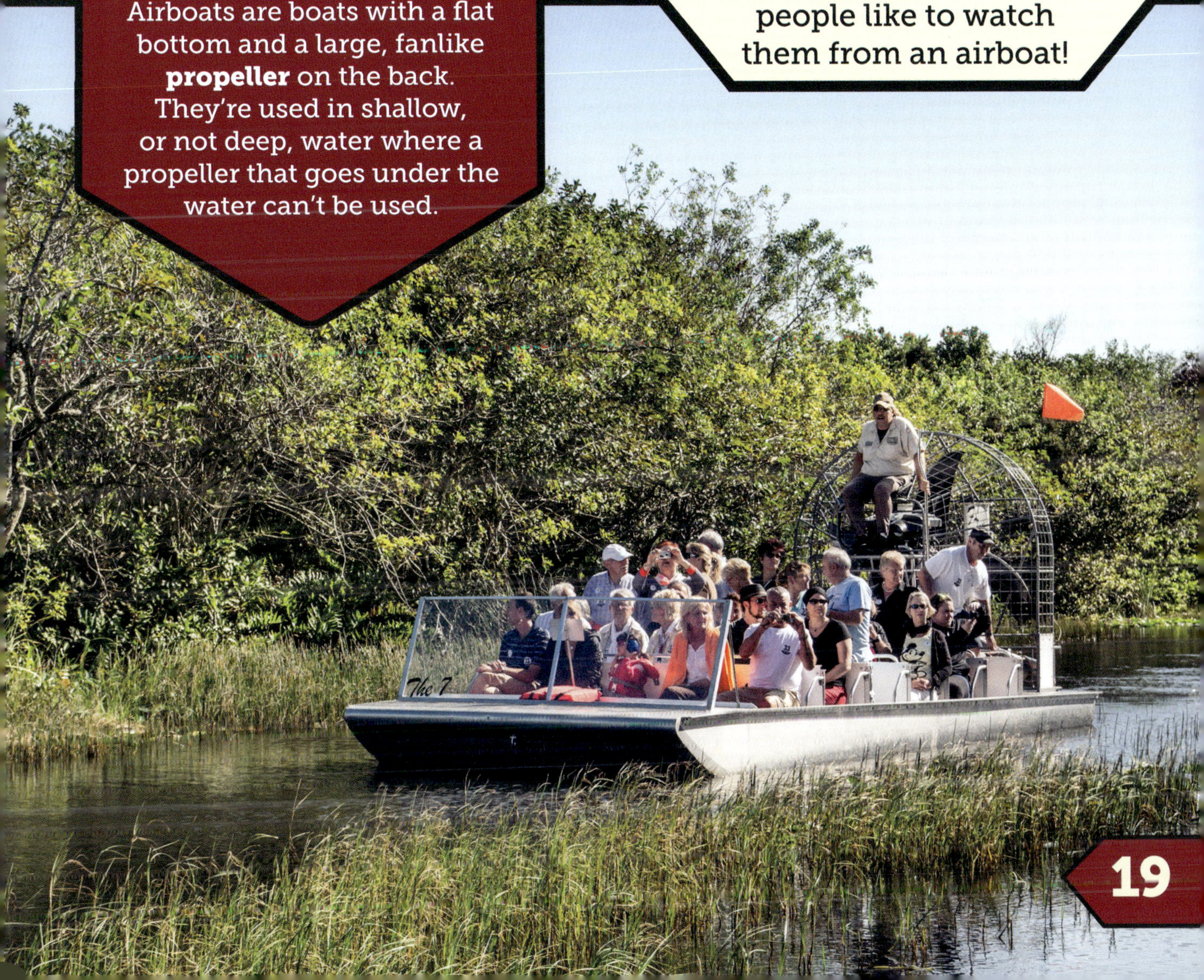

PLANNING YOUR VISIT

Everglades National Park is open all year. While you can visit any time of year you'd like, the best time to visit the Everglades is during its dry season. This is from December to April. The temperature in the park is cooler and usually only reaches 77°F (25°C) or so.

If you go during the dry season, you may run into crowds! The dry season is the busiest time of year for the Everglades National Park.

MORE TO KNOW

Make sure to pack your bug spray. While bugs like mosquitoes aren't as common during the dry season, they still bite all year!

EVERGLADES NATIONAL PARK

THE FACTS

ESTABLISHED
1934 (didn't open until 1947)

SIZE
2,400 square miles (6,216 sq km)

NUMBER OF VISITORS EACH YEAR
around 1 million

NATIVE WILDLIFE
alligators, manatees, Florida panthers, tree frogs, and more

NATIVE PLANTS
orchids, water lilies, mangroves, and more

MUST-SEE STOPS
Mahogany Hammock Trail, Everglades Safari Park, Shark Valley

GLOSSARY

breed: To come together to have babies.

conservationist: Someone who works to care for the natural world.

ecosystem: A natural community of living and nonliving things.

habitat: The natural home for plants, animals, and other living things.

inland: Toward the inside of land away from the water.

invasive: Describing plants or animals from one area that spread quickly in a new area and harm native plants and animals.

monitor: To watch carefully.

propeller: Parts on a ship or boat that spin in the water to move the ship or boat forward.

restore: To bring something back to the way it was before.

subtropical: An area near the warm part of Earth close to the equator.

swamp: An area with trees that is covered with water at least part of the time.

unique: One of a kind.

FOR YOUR INFORMATION

Books

Jacobson, Bray. *The Everglades*. Buffalo, NY: Gareth Stevens Publishing, 2023.

Nelson, Penelope. *Everglades National Park*. Minneapolis, MN: Jump!, 2020.

Websites

National Geographic Kids: Everglades National Park
www.kids.nationalgeographic.com/nature/article/everglades
Learn more about Everglades National Park.

National Park Service: Everglades National Park Florida
www.nps.gov/ever/learn/kidsyouth/index.htm
Discover things you can do during your visit to Everglades National Park.

INDEX